TOOLS FOR CAREGIVERS

- **F&P LEVEL:** C
- **WORD COUNT:** 29
- **CURRICULUM CONNECTIONS:** holidays, traditions

Skills to Teach

- **HIGH-FREQUENCY WORDS:** a, I, is, it, see
- **CONTENT WORDS:** art, day, food, fun, green, have, make, parade, Patrick's, river, St., wear
- **PUNCTUATION:** exclamation points, periods
- **WORD STUDY:** long /a/, spelled ay (day); long /e/, spelled ee (green, see); /oo/, spelled oo (food)
- **TEXT TYPE:** information report

Before Reading Activities

- Read the title and give a simple statement of the main idea.
- Have students "walk" through the book and talk about what they see in the pictures.
- Introduce new vocabulary by having students predict the first letter and locate the word in the text.
- Discuss any unfamiliar concepts that are in the text.

After Reading Activities

Flip back through the book with readers. Ask them to name the color of St. Patrick's Day. Then ask them to think of other holiday colors. Have readers draw a symbol from their favorite holiday and color it with the holiday's colors.

Tadpole Books are published by Jump!, 5357 Penn Avenue South, Minneapolis, MN 55419, www.jumplibrary.com

Copyright ©2025 Jump!. International copyright reserved in all countries. No part of this book may be reproduced in any form without written permission from the publisher.

Editor: Alyssa Sorenson **Designer:** Molly Ballanger

Photo Credits: skodonnell/iStock, cover; glenda/Shutterstock, 1; gpointstudio/iStock, 2tl, 12–13, 16; Slawomir Fajer/Shutterstock, 2tr, 4–5; Shutterstock, 2ml, 14–15; Blulz60/Shutterstock, 2mr, 8–9; Tzido/iStock, 2br, 6–7; jlmatt/iStock, 2bl, 10–11; New Africa/Shutterstock, 3.

Library of Congress Cataloging-in-Publication Data
Names: Austen, Lily, author.
Title: St. Patrick's Day / by Lily Austen.
Other titles: Saint Patrick's Day
Description: Minneapolis, MN: Jump!, Inc., [2025]
Series: Holiday fun! | Includes index.
Audience: Ages 3–6
Identifiers: LCCN 2024019236 (print)
LCCN 2024019237 (ebook)
ISBN 9798892135108 (hardcover)
ISBN 9798892135115 (paperback)
ISBN 9798892135122 (ebook)
Subjects: LCSH: Saint Patrick's Day—Juvenile literature.
Patrick, Saint, 373?–463?—Juvenile literature.
Classification: LCC GT4995.P3 A97 2025 (print)
LCC GT4995.P3 (ebook)
DDC 394.262—dc23/eng/20240429
LC record available at https://lccn.loc.gov/2024019236
LC ebook record available at https://lccn.loc.gov/2024019237

HOLIDAY FUN!
ST. PATRICK'S DAY

by Lily Austen

TABLE OF CONTENTS

Words to Know 2

St. Patrick's Day 3

Let's Review! 16

Index 16

WORDS TO KNOW

art

food

fun

parade

river

wear

ST. PATRICK'S DAY

It is St. Patrick's Day!

I see food.

I see a parade!

I wear green.

I make art.

LET'S REVIEW!

St. Patrick's Day is March 17. It celebrates Irish culture. How is this family celebrating?

INDEX

art 13
food 5
fun 15

green 7, 11
parade 9
river 7